A Child's
First Catholic
Dictionary

Richard W. Dyches & Thomas Mustachio
Illustrations by Ansgar Holmberg, C.S.J.

AVE MARIA PRESS Notre Dame, Indiana 46556

For Katie and Matt

© 1994 by Ave Maria Press, Inc., Notre Dame, IN 46556

International Standard Book Number: 0-87793-525-4

Library of Congress Catalog Card Number: 94-71885

Cover and text design by Elizabeth J. French

Printed and bound in the United States of America.

Dear Parent and Teacher,

A Child's First Catholic Dictionary is a one-of-a-kind book.

Its clear and concise definitions coupled with lively and provocative illustrations will both inform and entertain. Children will love exploring its illustrations as they learn the meaning of age-old Catholic terms and concepts.

Although developed with the six- through nine-year-old in mind, older children and adults will also find the 252 definitions and full-color illustrations enjoyable and useful.

With each picture a story in itself, we hope you will find it a book you can enjoy with your children again and again. We believe its words and illustrations will spark thought-provoking dialogue as you explore important ideas and stories of the Catholic faith with them.

A Child's First Catholic Dictionary provides the first important step in religious literacy and helps to make the story of faith accessible to all children. With the use of this important catechetical tool, we are confident that children will learn and feel more comfortable with the religious terminology so necessary to grow in their faith and their relationship with God.

Richard W Dyches

Thomas G. Mustachio

Richard Dyches is a consultant and writer of educational materials for children of all ages. Among his books are the *First Math Dictionary*, *First Science Dictionary*, and *Helping Your Child at Home with Mathematics*. A former elementary teacher and college professor, Dyches is a frequent lecturer at national and international workshops and conferences.

Thomas Mustachio is an educational consultant, graphic designer, and musician who has worked as a religious educator and church musician for over twenty years. He has composed a great deal of church music and has organized and directed many children's and adult choirs. He presents seminars and workshops in church music.

Ansgar Holmberg's striking and colorful art appears in various religious publications including *Catechist* magazine. A former elementary school teacher, she is currently a member of a team involved with adult spiritual growth programs at the Loyola Center in St. Paul, MN.

Abba

Abba means "daddy." Because Jesus called God **"Abba"** Christians often think of God as their father in heaven.

Abraham

You shall have as many descendants as there are stars in the sky

Abraham and his wife Sarah, whose stories are told in the Old Testament, are respected by Jews, Christians, and Moslems. All three religions trace their history to them.

absolution

To **absolve** means "to wash." After we confess our sins to the priest, he says the prayer of **absolution** as a sign that our sins are forgiven.

Act of Contrition

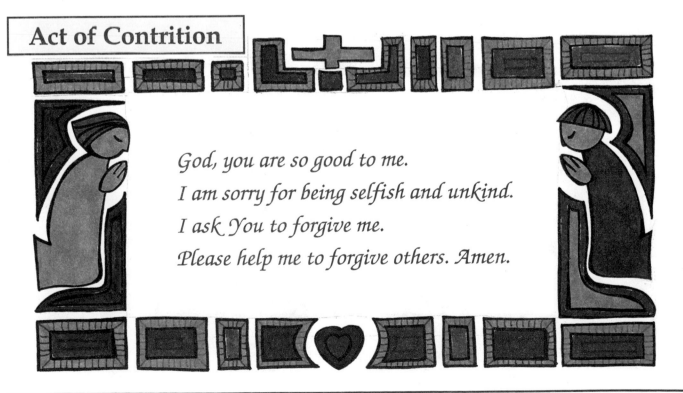

God, you are so good to me.
I am sorry for being selfish and unkind.
I ask You to forgive me.
Please help me to forgive others. Amen.

An **Act of Contrition** is a prayer we say to tell God how sorry we are for our sins.

Aa

Adam and Eve

Adam and Eve were the first humans created by God. They lived in the Garden of Eden.

Advent

Advent means "coming." **Advent** is the church season four weeks before Christmas, when we get ready for Jesus' birthday.

alb

An **alb** is the long, white robe worn by priests or other ministers when they lead a public prayer. The word **alb** means "white."

All Saints' Day

November 1 is **All Saints' Day**. This is when we thank God for the lives and examples of all holy people.

All Souls' Day

November 2 is **All Souls' Day**. This is the feast when the church remembers and prays for all people who have died.

Alleluia

Alleluia is a joyful word that means "Praise God!" It is shouted or sung.

altar

An **altar** is a table in church where the priest and people gather to celebrate the Mass.

Amen

We thank you, God, for your Kindness to us.

Amen.

Amen.

Amen means "Yes! Let it be so!" When you speak, sing, or shout **"Amen,"** it means that you agree with what has been said.

angel

Angels are spirits created to love and praise God. They help God to care for people. The word **angel** means "messenger."

Annunciation, Feast of the

On March 25, the church celebrates the **Feast of the Annunciation**. This is the day when the angel Gabriel told Mary that she was going to be the Mother of God.

Anointing of the Sick

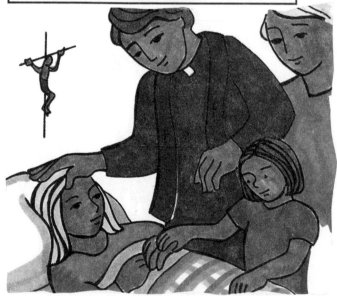

Anointing of the Sick is a sacrament of healing. When someone is sick, the community prays for them and the priest anoints or rubs oil of the sick on them. These are signs of God's love and care.

apostle

An **apostle** is a special helper of Jesus. Jesus chose twelve **apostles** and sent them to preach, heal, and teach in his name.

Aa

Apostles' Creed

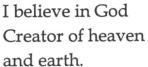

I believe in God
Creator of heaven
and earth.

I believe in Jesus Christ,
Son of God,
Born of Mary.
He lived, suffered,
died and was buried.
He rose again
and is with his Father, God.

I believe in
the Holy Catholic
    church,
the communion of
    saints,
the forgiveness of sins,
the resurrection of
the body
and life everlasting.

YES!
AMEN!

The **Apostles' Creed** is a prayer of our Catholic beliefs. In praying it we voice a faith that we share with the first apostles.

10

Ascension, Feast of the

The **Feast of the Ascension** is on a Thursday, forty days after Easter. It is the day we celebrate Jesus' return to God in heaven.

Ash Wednesday

Ash Wednesday begins the season of Lent. We receive ashes on our foreheads as a sign that we are sorry for our sins.

Assumption, Feast of the

The **Feast of the Assumption** is on August 15. This is the day the church celebrates Mary being taken to heaven to live with Jesus.

Baptism

Baptism is a sacrament of belonging. A minister baptizes people by pouring water over their foreheads and blessing them in the name of the Father, and of the Son, and of the Holy Spirit.

Baptism of Jesus

Jesus was baptized by John the Baptist in the River Jordan. A voice from heaven proclaimed that Jesus was God's Son.

baptismal font

A **baptismal font** is the container for the water which is used at baptism.

Beatitudes

> Blessed are the merciful.
> Blessed are the peacemakers.
> Blessed are those who mourn.

The **Beatitudes** are some short sayings that Jesus taught in the Sermon on the Mount. They describe good ways to live and be happy.

Bethlehem

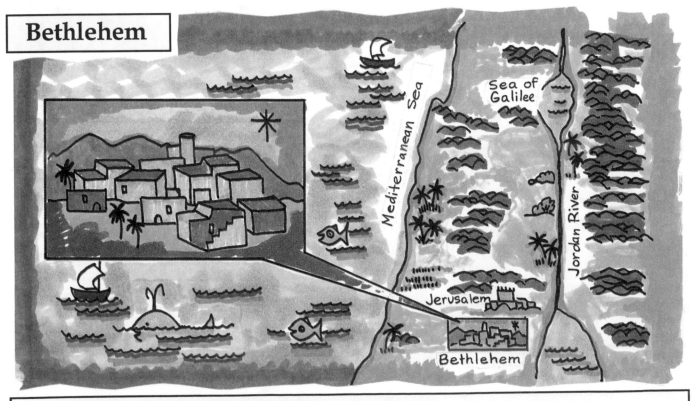

Bethlehem is the town in Judea where Jesus was born.

Bible

THE OLD TESTAMENT

THE NEW TESTAMENT

The beginning of the good news of Jesus Christ, the Son of God

Then Moses and the Israelites sang this song to the Lord: "I will sing to the Lord, for he has triumphed gloriously; horse and rider he has thrown into the sea.

The word **Bible** means "book." The **Bible** is the word of God, and is actually made up of many books written by different authors. God chose them to tell the story of God's life with people on earth.

bishop

A **bishop** is a person chosen to look after and care for God's people in an area called a diocese.

Blessed Mother

Jesus said "This is your mother."

Blessed Mother is another name for Mary. She is blessed, or gifted, because she is the Mother of God and our mother too.

blessings

Blessings, like food, family, and love, are the gifts God has given to us. A **blessing** is also the name of a prayer that asks for God's love and care.

Body of Christ

As members of the church, we are part of the **Body of Christ**.
We also call the blessed bread at eucharist the **Body of Christ**.

bread

Bread is a food which helps us grow and gives us strength.
Jesus is called the **Bread of Life** because his love does the
same thing for us.

Cc

Calvary

Calvary is a hill near the city of Jerusalem. **Calvary** is the place where Jesus was hung on a wooden cross to die.

candles

Candles give off beautiful light. They are used at Mass to remind us of Jesus' presence in the world and in the gifts of bread and wine.

care

To **care** for someone is to love them and want them to be well and happy. We **care** for our families and friends.

catechist

A **catechist** is someone who teaches others about God and God's word.

catholic

The word **catholic** means "for everyone." The **Catholic** church is a church that is open to all people.

Cc

celebrant

The people who lead our church worship services are called **celebrants** because they help everyone to celebrate the love of God.

celebrate

To **celebrate** means to have a good time. We **celebrate** at religious services like the Mass because we are happy that God loves us.

chalice

A **chalice** is a cup. When we receive holy communion we drink wine from a **chalice**.

chapel

A **chapel** is a place of worship and prayer that is smaller than a church. Chapels are found in buildings like hospitals and schools.

charity

Charity is another word for Christian love. We show **charity** when we are kind to other people. When we give help to someone in need, we are being **charitable**.

chasuble

A **chasuble** is the colorful outer garment worn by the celebrant of Mass. It is usually green, white, violet, or red, depending on the season or day in the Church Year.

choir

A **choir** is a group of people who sing together. **Choirs** can have many members or just a few.

chrism

Chrism is holy oil blessed by the bishop. It is made of olive oil and perfume, and smells sweet. When you are baptized and confirmed you are anointed with **chrism**.

Cc

Christ

Christ means "the Chosen One." Jesus is the **Christ**, because he is the one chosen by God to save the world from sin.

Christian

A **Christian** is someone who is a baptized follower of Jesus Christ. **Christians** try to live as Jesus lived, loving God and all God's people.

Christmas

On December 25 we celebrate the birth of Jesus Christ. We call this **Christmas** Day.

church

The **church** is the name for the people of God on earth. It is also called the Body of Christ. The word **church** can also be used to name the building we worship in.

Church Year

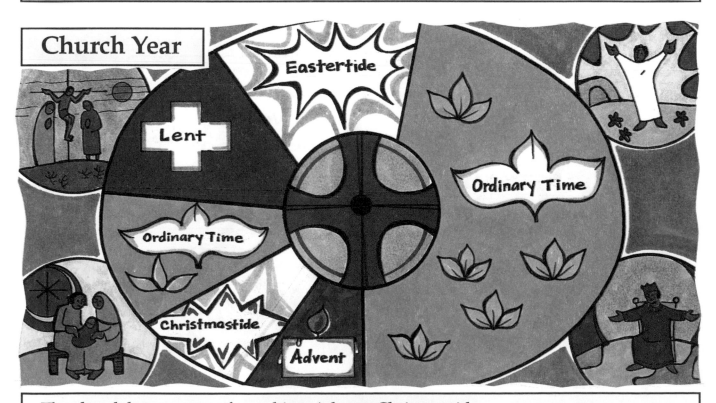

The church has seasons of worship—Advent, Christmastide, Lent, Eastertide, and Ordinary Time. The **Church Year** includes these seasons plus many other special days.

ciborium

A **ciborium** is a covered container for keeping the blessed hosts after Mass.

clergy

The **clergy** are the people who have received the sacrament of Holy Orders. **Clergy** serve the people of God as bishops, priests, or deacons.

commandment

Love God with all your heart

Love your neighbor as yourself

A **commandment** is a law that helps people to follow God. Jesus gave us two great **commandments**: *Love God with all your heart* and *Love your neighbor as yourself.*

communion of saints

The **communion of saints** is the family of all Christians, both living and dead.

community

A **community** is a group of people who have something in common. The church is called a **community** of faith because its members believe the same things about Jesus Christ and follow his example.

confess

When we **confess**, we admit something we have done is wrong. In the sacrament of Reconciliation we **confess** our sins to a priest.

Confirmation

wisdom right judgment
understanding Knowledge
courage reverence
wonder and
awe

Confirmation is a sacrament of belonging or initiation. At **Confirmation** we receive the gifts of the Holy Spirit.

conscience

Our **conscience** is our ability to know what is right or wrong. When we choose to do the right thing we are using our **conscience**.

consecration

Consecration means "to make holy." At Mass, the priest prays a special blessing **consecrating** bread and wine into the body and blood of Jesus.

contrition

God, I am sorry.

Contrition is a feeling of sorrow for any wrong we may have done. When we feel **contrition** we want to try to do better in the future.

conversion

Conversion is a change from one way of life to another. It is also when we recognize that God loves us and we accept the teachings of the church.

covenant

I am your God

We are your people

A **covenant** is a holy promise between God and people. Testament is another word for **covenant**.

creation

Creation is everything—people, animals, and nature. God **created** everything.

Creator

A **creator** is someone who makes things. We believe that God is the **Creator** who made *all* things.

creed

A **creed** is a belief or a list of what a community believes.

cross

Because Jesus died on a **cross**, it is the main symbol of the Christian faith.

crucifix

A **crucifix** is a cross with a figure of Christ on it.

Dd

deacon

A **deacon** is an ordained minister who serves the community by caring for the sick, poor, and elderly.

death

For Christians, **death** is the end of life on this earth and the beginning of life in heaven with God.

Dd

diocese

A **diocese** is an area that includes people and parishes under the care of a bishop.

disciple

A **disciple** is a person who learns from Jesus and follows him.

divine

Anything connected with God is **divine**. God's love is **divine** love.

dove

A **dove** is often used as a symbol for the Holy Spirit—God's love. The **dove** is also a symbol for peace.

Easter

Easter is the feast when we celebrate Jesus' resurrection.

Emmanuel

Emmanuel means "God is with us." **Emmanuel** is also another name for Jesus.

Epiphany, Feast of the

The **Feast of the Epiphany** is the second Sunday after Christmas. It is the day we remember the visit of the wise men to Jesus. The wise men saw and believed that Jesus was God's Son.

33

epistle

The Letter of Paul to the ROMANS

To all God's beloved in Rome, who are called to be saints:

Grace to you and peace from God our Father and the Lord Jesus Christ.

First, I thank my God through Jesus Christ for all of you, because your faith is proclaimed throughout the world. For God, whom I serve with my spirit by announcing the gospel.

An **epistle** is a letter. Some books of the Bible are called **epistles**. They are letters of encouragement from the disciples of Jesus to Christians everywhere.

eternal

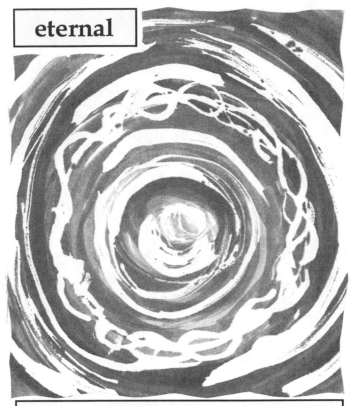

Eternal means "forever." Something without beginning or end is **eternal**. God is **eternal**.

Eucharist

Eucharist is the sacrament of the body and blood of Jesus.
Eucharist is the Greek word for "thanksgiving."

evangelists

Evangelists are people who speak or write about the good news of Christ. In the Bible, the authors of the gospels of Matthew, Mark, Luke, and John are called the four **evangelists**.

everlasting life

Jesus promises us **everlasting life**, or life without end, if we believe in him.

Ee

evil

Anything bad or wrong which causes us to sin is **evil**. The devil is **evil**.

examination of conscience

What am I grateful for today?
What am I sorry for?
What did I do well today?

An **examination of conscience** is a time when we try to remember any wrong things we have done so that we can try to change our bad habits. It is part of the sacrament of Reconciliation.

Exodus

Exodus is a Greek word that means "going forth." The **Exodus** took place when the Hebrew people left their life of slavery in Egypt to go forth to Canaan, the land of freedom.

faith

Faith is believing and trusting in God's love. **Faith** is a gift from God that we experience as members of the church.

family

Families come in all sizes, some with two parents and many children, some with only one parent and child. But God's **family** is enormous and we are all part of it as brothers and sisters to one another.

Ff

fast

To **fast** means "to go without food or with little food for a period of time." Catholics sometimes **fast** during the season of Lent as a way to feel closer to the poor and hungry.

Father

Jesus called God **"Father"** to show that God loves us as a parent loves a child. God the **Father** is the first person of the Blessed Trinity.

feast day

A **feast day** is a holy day in the Church Year when we remember and think about a saint or special event. Christmas and Easter are **feast days**.

forgiveness

Forgiveness is when we become friends with someone we have hurt or who has hurt us. God always offers **forgiveness** when we have done wrong.

Gg

general intercessions

Let us pray for
the leaders of our church.

Let us pray for those
who are sick.

Let us pray for those
who suffer from war.

Lord, hear our prayer.

The **general intercessions** are the prayers which people offer at Mass for their needs and the needs of others. They are also called the Prayers of the Faithful.

Genesis

GENESIS
In the beginning when God created the heavens and the earth, the earth was a formless void and darkness covered the face of the deep while a wind from God

Genesis means "beginning." The book of **Genesis** is the first book of the Bible. It tells the story of the beginning of the world.

genuflect

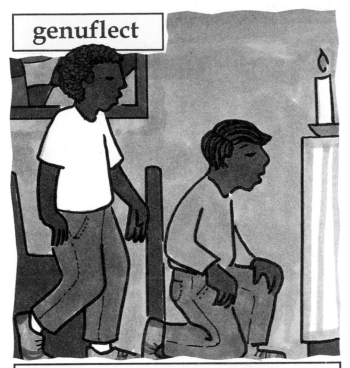

We **genuflect** by touching our right knee to the ground and standing back up. It is a sign of respect we show when we enter and leave the presence of Jesus in church.

gifts

Gifts are things we give freely without wanting to get something in return. God freely gives love to all people. Jesus freely gave his life on the cross so that all people could be saved.

God

God is the Creator—the source of all life. **God** will never stop loving us. Christians believe in one **God** who is three persons: Father, Son, and Holy Spirit.

godparents

Godparents are the people who sponsor or speak for us at Baptism. They promise to pray for us and our parents.

Good Friday

Holy Thursday

Good Friday

Holy Saturday

Easter Sunday

Good Friday is the Friday before Easter. It is the day we remember that Jesus died on the cross. It is called **"good"** because we are saved through Jesus' death.

Good Samaritan

Jesus tells a story about a good person from the land of Samaria who helped a stranger in need. A person who helps others is sometimes called a **"Good Samaritan."**

Good Shepherd

A **good shepherd** watches over and cares for the sheep. Jesus is called the **Good Shepherd** because he watches over and cares for us.

gospel

Gospel means "good news." The New Testament books of Matthew, Mark, Luke, and John are the four **gospels**. They tell the good news of the words and actions of Jesus Christ.

grace

Grace is a share of God's own life and goodness. **Grace** is a gift of God, given at Baptism.

grace at meals

Grace at meals is a prayer or blessing that people share before eating. We ask God to bless both the food and those who are about to share it.

43

Hh

Hail Mary

Hail Mary, full of grace,
the Lord is with you.
Blessed are you among women,
and blessed is the fruit
  of your womb, Jesus.

Holy Mary,
Mother of God,
pray for us sinners,
now and at the hour
  of our death. Amen

"Hail, Mary" was the way the angel Gabriel greeted Mary at the annunciation. **Hail** is a respectful way of saying "hello." The **Hail Mary** is a prayer which begins with Gabriel's greeting.

heaven

Heaven is life in God's presence forever.

Hebrew Scriptures

Another name for the Old Testament books of the Bible is the **Hebrew Scriptures**. These books were the sacred writings of the Hebrew people.

hell

Hell is being separated from God and God's love forever.

Hh

holy

Holy means "being like God." People are **holy** when they live like Jesus.

holy days

All Saints
Ascension
Assumption
Christmas
Immaculate Conception
Solemnity of Mary

Holy days are days in the Church Year when we remember special events in the life of Jesus or Mary. Catholics attend Mass on **holy days**.

Holy Family

The **Holy Family** is Jesus, his mother Mary, and her husband Joseph.

Holy Land

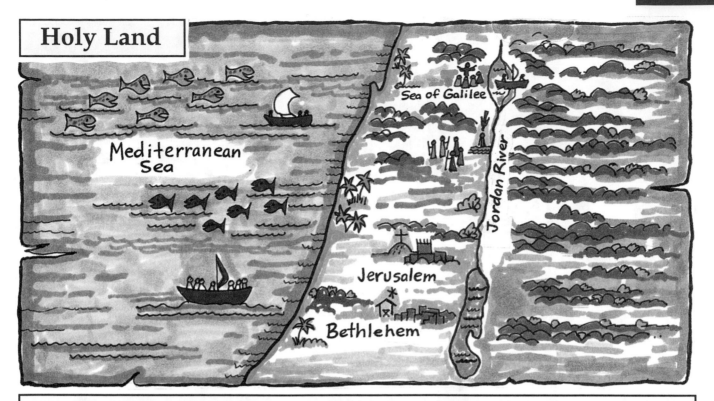

The land of Israel where Jesus was born and lived is called
the **Holy Land**.

Holy Spirit

The **Holy Spirit** is the helper Jesus promised to send to his
friends when he went to join his Father in heaven. The **Holy
Spirit** is the third person of the Blessed Trinity.

Hh

Holy Thursday

Holy Thursday is the Thursday before Easter. This is when Jesus shared his Last Supper with his friends and washed their feet. On **Holy Thursday,** we celebrate Jesus' gift of the Eucharist and his call to serve others.

holy water

Water which is blessed by a priest is **holy water**. It is used by Christians to remind them of their Baptism.

Holy Week

Palm Sunday
Monday
Tuesday
Wednesday
Holy Thursday
Good Friday
Holy Saturday

Holy Week is the week before Easter. It begins on Palm Sunday. During **Holy Week** we remember that Jesus suffered and died for us.

48

homily

A **homily** is a brief talk about the meaning of the Bible readings shared at Mass.

honesty

Honesty means being truthful. Jesus taught us not to lie but to be **honest**.

hope

To **hope** is to believe that God's love will always be with us. At Baptism, we are given the gift of **hope**.

Hosanna

Hosanna means "Praise be to God." The crowd of people shouted **"Hosanna"** and waved palms as Jesus rode into Jerusalem on a donkey.

host

The **host** is the bread we eat during the celebration of the Eucharist. When the **host** is blessed at Mass, it is the Body of Christ.

hymn

A **hymn** is a song of praise to God. We sing **hymns** at church and at home.

Immaculate Conception, Feast of the

Mary, the Mother of God, was free from sin from the first moment of her life. The church calls this the **Immaculate Conception** and celebrates the feast on December 8.

incarnation

Incarnation is the belief that God became human when Jesus was born of his mother Mary.

incense

Incense is a mixture of perfumes and spices which gives off sweet-smelling smoke. **Incense** is often used when we pray, to remind us that our prayers rise to God as smoke rises to the sky.

inspiration

Inspiration means "in the spirit." The writers of the Bible were **inspired** by the Holy Spirit to put the words and ideas God wanted into their writings.

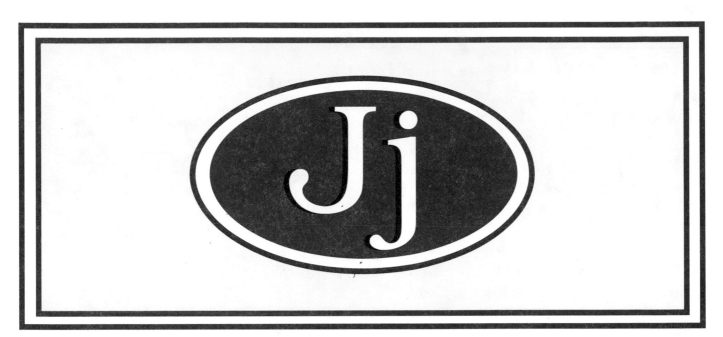

Jj

Jerusalem

Jerusalem, also known as Zion, is the Holy City for the Jewish people. **Jerusalem** is holy for Christians also, because Jesus spent much of his time there and was crucified outside the city walls.

Jesus, the Christ

Jesus means "God saves." It is the name which the angel Gabriel told Mary to name her child, the Son of God. His followers added **"Christ"** because they believed that **Jesus** was God's Chosen One.

Jj

Jesus Prayer

The words of the **Jesus Prayer** are "Lord Jesus Christ, Son of God, have mercy on me." When we say these words over and over, they help us feel closer to God.

Jew

A **Jew** is a member of an ancient religion called Judaism. Thousands of years ago God was made known to the **Jews** whom God called the Chosen People. Jesus was a **Jew.**

John the Baptist

John the Baptist was a relative of Jesus who lived in the desert. Jesus asked **John the Baptist** to baptize him. **John** baptized Jesus in the Jordan River.

Joseph

Joseph, in the New Testament, was the husband of Mary. He helped Mary raise God's Son, Jesus. **Joseph** was Jesus' foster father.

joy

Joy is great happiness. Our faith in Jesus and his promises brings us **joy**.

justice

Justice is fair treatment. We are **just** when we try to provide for the most basic needs of all people.

Kk Ll

The **laity** is the name for all baptized people who have not been ordained.

Lamb of God

The **Lamb of God** is a name for Jesus. It shows us how gentle and loving Jesus is.

56

Last Supper

The **Last Supper** was the meal Jesus ate with his disciples the night before he died. Jesus changed bread and wine into his body and blood. The **Last Supper** is remembered as the first Mass.

lectionary

The **lectionary** is the book that contains the Bible stories read at Mass.

lector

A **lector** is a person who reads from the Bible at Mass during the Liturgy of the Word.

Lent

	Sunday	Monday	Tuesday	Wednesday	Thursday	Friday	Saturday
1							
2							
3							
4							
5							
6							

Lent is the season of prayer and penance before Easter. It begins on Ash Wednesday and continues for forty days.

liturgical colors

Easter
Pentecost
Lent
Advent
Christmas
Ordinary Time

Liturgical colors are the colors that have special meaning for a season of the Church Year or for a church feast. For example, white is a color of joy and new life and is used at Easter. Other **liturgical colors** are violet (Advent and Lent), red (Pentecost), green (Ordinary Time), and blue (Mary's feast days).

liturgy

Liturgy means "public worship." Celebrations of the Eucharist and the other sacraments are examples of **liturgy**.

Liturgy of the Eucharist

The **Liturgy of the Eucharist** is the part of the Mass when we remember and give thanks for Jesus' gift of his body and blood.

59

Liturgy of the Hours

The **Liturgy of the Hours** is the daily prayer of the church. It is also known as the "Divine Office." The **Liturgy of the Hours** is prayed by reading scripture at different times from early morning to late night.

Liturgy of the Word

The **Liturgy of the Word** is the part of the Mass when we hear God's word read from scripture and explained in the homily.

Lord

Lord is a title of respect. When we call Jesus **Lord**, we mean that he is God.

Lord's Day

Sunday is known as the **Lord's Day**. On this day we worship the Lord by celebrating the Eucharist. It is also called the Sabbath.

61

KkLl

Lord's Supper

The **Lord's Supper** is a name Christians use to describe the celebration of the Eucharist.

love

Love is another word for God. We **love** others when we show that we want what is best for them. This shows we belong to God.

Mm

Magnificat

My soul gives praise to you, O my God, and my spirit rejoices in you. For you have blessed me. From this day all peoples will call me blessed.

Magnificat is the song Jesus' mother Mary sang when she visited her cousin, Elizabeth. The words of the **Magnificat** tell of God's greatness.

Mm

manger

A **manger** is a feeding box for farm animals. When Jesus was born in the stable in Bethlehem, Joseph and Mary laid him in a **manger**.

marks of the church

The **marks of the church** are words that describe what the church is and should be. These four words are: one, holy, catholic, and apostolic.

marriage

Marriage is a sacrament celebrating the commitment of a man and woman to love one another forever, raise a family, and serve the church.

martyr

Martyr means "witness." A **martyr** is a person who has been killed for living his or her religious beliefs.

Mary, Mother of God

Mary is the **Mother of God** because she gave birth to Jesus, God's Son.

Mass

Mass is a name for the Eucharist. It is a time when Catholics gather to hear God's word and celebrate the Eucharist.

mercy

Father, forgive them, they do not know what they are doing.

Mercy is an act of forgiveness. We show **mercy** when we are forgiving and willing to help others in need.

Messiah

Messiah is the Hebrew word for Christ, "the Chosen One."

minister

A **minister** is a servant. Parish **ministers** serve people in many ways—by reading God's word, giving communion, or visiting the sick.

ministry

Ministry means "using our time and talents to serve God and others."

Mm

miracle

Jesus cured the eyes
of a man born blind.

Jesus gave life to a
girl who died.

Jesus healed sick
people who came to him.

A **miracle** is a wonderful and unexpected event which shows
God's power and love. Jesus performed many **miracles** to
show people he had been sent by God.

mission

A **mission** is a job or task. Jesus sent his apostles on a **mission**. to preach, teach, and heal in his name. The church's **mission** is to spread the good news of Jesus Christ.

missionary

A **missionary** is anyone who is sent to share the gospel with others.

Mm

monastery

A **monastery** is a home for a religious community of men called monks.

Moses

Moses was the most important leader of the Old Testament. He led the people of Israel out of Egypt and received God's Law in the desert. Jesus is called the New **Moses**.

mystery

A **mystery** is an event which we cannot completely understand. A mystery may be connected with the life of Christ. Jesus' incarnation is a **mystery**.

Nn

Nativity

The **Nativity** is the birth of Jesus Christ in the town of Bethlehem.

Nazareth

Nazareth is the town in Galilee where Joseph, Mary, and Jesus lived.

New Covenant

The **New Covenant** expresses the promise of God's friendship with the followers of Jesus. God promises that we will live forever.

Noah

The Bible describes **Noah** as a good man who built an ark in order to save his family and the animals from a great flood.

Oo

oil of the sick

Oil of the sick is a special oil, blessed by the bishop. This oil is used to anoint people who are old or very sick.

ordination

Ordination is the sacrament that celebrates the promise of a deacon, priest or bishop to serve the People of God.

original sin

Original sin is the separation between God and people that began when Adam and Eve chose to disobey God. Jesus' life and death freed humans from the effects of **original sin**.

Our Father

Our Father, who art in heaven,

hallowed be Your name.

Your kingdom come,

Your will be done

on earth as it is in heaven.

Give us this day our daily bread.

Forgive us our trespasses

as we forgive those

who trespass against us.

Lead us not into temptation,

but deliver us from evil.

Amen.

Jesus taught his friends a prayer which begins with the words
"Our Father …" We also call it the Lord's Prayer.

Our Lady of Guadalupe

In 1531 Mary appeared to a poor Mexican man, Juan Diego, and told him to ask his bishop to build a church on the site. The bishop asked for a sign. It was winter and Juan found roses growing where Mary appeared and her picture imprinted on his cloak. The church was built and pilgrims have visited it ever since. We celebrate the feast of **Our Lady of Guadalupe** on December 12.

Palm Sunday

Palm Sunday, also called Passion Sunday, is the Sunday before Easter. On **Palm Sunday**, we carry palm leaves in church. This reminds us that Jesus entered Jerusalem to the cheers of people who waved palm branches and called him king.

Pp

parable

A father had two sons. He asked one son to go work in his vineyard

The son said, "Yes" but he didn't do it.

The father asked the other son to go work. The son said, "No, I won't" but he went after all.

Which child was the good son?

A **parable** is a story that teaches an important lesson. Jesus used **parables** to teach lessons about how people should live their lives. A famous **parable** is the story of the Good Samaritan.

parish

A **parish** is a community of people who come together to worship God and to serve the needs of others.

Paschal Mystery

The **Paschal Mystery** is the death and resurrection of Jesus.

passion

The **passion** is Jesus' arrest, trial, suffering, and death. We remember these events on Good Friday.

Pp

Passover

The **Passover** is a feast in which Jewish people recall how God saved their ancestors from slavery in Egypt.

pastor

Pastor means "shepherd." Leaders of parishes are called **pastors** because they care for their people as shepherds care for their sheep.

Paul

Paul was a preacher and missionary in the early church. Some of the letters he wrote to help early Christians are part of the Bible.

peace

Peace is a gift from God that helps bring calmness and goodness to ourselves and others.

penance

Penance is a prayer or a good deed we must do. **Penance** shows that we are sorry for a sin and that we want to do better. It is also another name for the sacrament of Reconciliation.

penitential rite

Lord, have mercy on us.

Christ, have mercy on us.

The **penitential rite** occurs at the beginning of the Mass. This is when we tell God that we have not lived as we should. We ask for mercy and forgiveness from God and the community.

Pentecost

Pentecost means "fiftieth day." Fifty days after Easter the apostles were filled with the Holy Spirit and went out to share the good news of Jesus. **Pentecost** is also the birthday of the church.

People of God

The members of the church are the **People of God**.

Peter

Peter was one of the twelve apostles. Jesus named him **Peter**, which means "rock," because he was to be the rock or foundation on which the church was built. **Peter** was the first pope.

pew

A **pew** is a bench. In many churches people sit on **pews** while they worship God.

Pp

pilgrimage

A **pilgrimage** is a journey people make to a sacred place.

pope

The **pope** is the bishop of Rome and head of the Roman Catholic church. He is the successor to Saint Peter. The word **pope** means "papa" in Latin.

praise

We Praise You

We Love You

Praise is a way to show how wonderful God is and how grateful we are to God. We can **praise** God in word or in song.

Pp

prayer

Prayer is talking and listening to God.

priest

A **priest** is an ordained minister who preaches God's word, celebrates the sacraments, and cares for God's people.

promised land

The **promised land** was the land of freedom that God promised to Moses and the Israelites.

Pp

prophet

A **prophet** is someone who speaks for God. **Prophets** call on people to love and serve others. Moses, his sister Miryam, and John the Baptist were **prophets**.

Protestant

FIRST CHRISTIAN CHURCH
SUNDAY SERVICE
10:00 A.M.
ALL WELCOME

A **Protestant** is a Christian who does not belong to the Catholic church.

psalm

PSALM 150

We praise you, O God, in your holy
   dwelling place;
We praise you in your mighty heavens;
We praise you according to your greatness.
We praise you with trumpet blast.
We praise you with strings and pipes.
We praise you with clashing cymbals.
Let everything that lives, praise you, O God!

A **psalm** is a song of praise to God. The Book of **Psalms** in the Bible includes 150 such songs.

Qq Rr

Reconciliation

Reconciliation is a sacrament. It celebrates God's gift of forgiveness and our return to God and the life of the church.

rectory

The place in a parish where priests live is called a **rectory**.

Redeemer

Redeemer is a name for Jesus Christ. It means he died to save us from our sins.

Reign of God

The **Reign of God** means that God actively takes part in our lives with the promise of making a better world for all people. Jesus began the **Reign of God** during his life on earth.

religious community

A **religious community** is a group of people who make promises to lead lives of prayer and service to God.

resurrection

The **resurrection** is Jesus' victory over sin and death by coming back to life.

revelation

Revelation is the way God's wishes for us are made known. The angel told Mary she would become God's Mother, **revealing** God's wishes to her.

ritual

A **ritual** is a set of words, actions, and gestures that we use to celebrate something special.

Rome

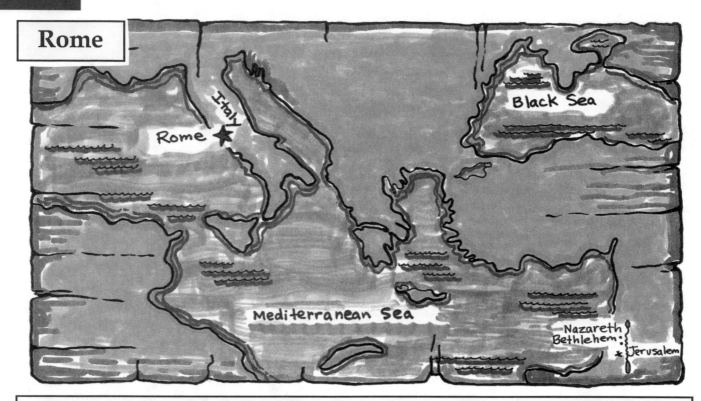

Rome is a large city in Italy. Because Saint Peter lived and died there, Peter's successor, the bishop of Rome, is the leader of the Roman Catholic church. He is called the pope.

Rosary

The **Rosary** is a group of prayers that help us remember events in the life of Jesus and Mary. We keep track of these prayers on a string of beads.

Ss

Sabbath

The **Sabbath** is the day of the week on which we rest and worship God. Catholics celebrate the **Sabbath** on Sunday, the day of Jesus' resurrection.

sacrament

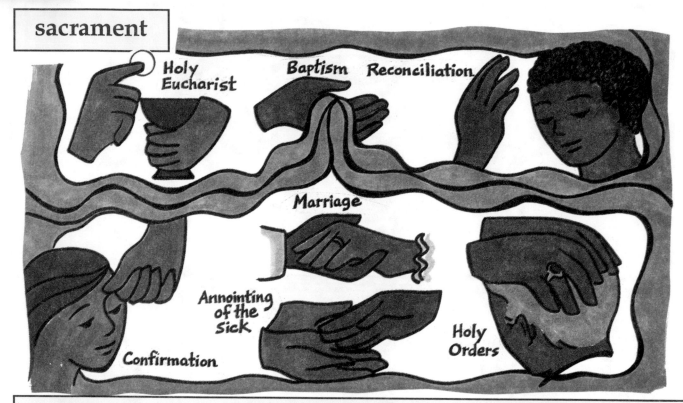

Holy
Eucharist

Baptism

Reconciliation

Marriage

Annointing
of the
Sick

Confirmation

Holy
Orders

A **sacrament** is a sign or symbol of God's love and presence.

sacramental

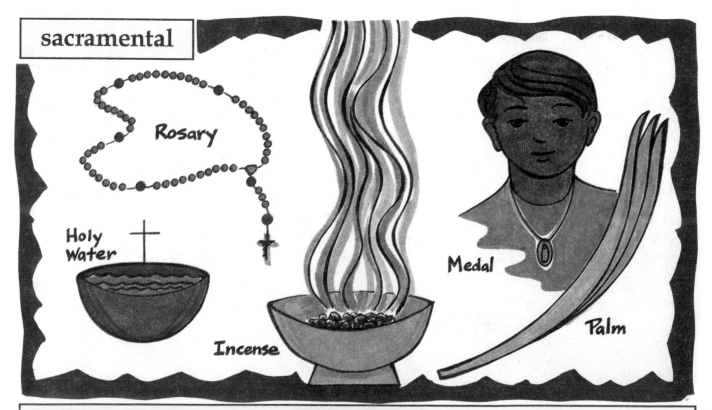

Rosary

Holy
Water

Incense

Medal

Palm

A **sacramental** is something that reminds us that God is near.
Religious pictures, rosary beads, holy water, and candles are
examples of **sacramentals**.

sacred

Sacred is another word for holy. Calvary is a **sacred** place because it is where Jesus died.

Sacred Heart

The **Sacred Heart** is the heart of Jesus. It is a symbol of his love for God and all people. Pictures and statues often show Jesus with his heart lit with the fire of love.

sacrifice

TOYS FOR THE HOMELESS CHILDREN

When we give up something we care for to help someone else, it is a **sacrifice**. Jesus' gift of his life on the cross is the perfect **sacrifice**.

saint

A **saint** is a Christian who lives as Jesus did. The church has named special **saints**. They were people who led very holy lives on earth and are now in heaven.

salt

Salt is a mineral that we take from the earth. Like water, we need **salt** for life. Jesus told his followers they were the "**salt** of the earth," meaning they were to bring goodness to the world and make it a better place.

salvation

We believe that Jesus is our **salvation.** He **saved** us from sin and death.

Satan

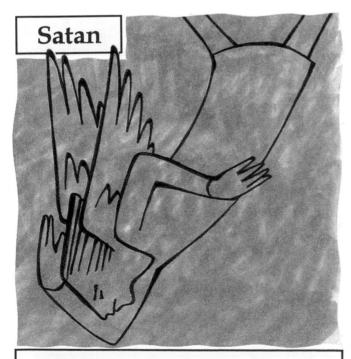

Satan is the name that Jesus gave to the tempter or devil who tries to keep us from loving God and doing what is right.

scripture

Scripture means "sacred writings." The books of the Bible are the **scriptures** used by Christians.

Sermon on the Mount

The **Sermon on the Mount** is a collection of Jesus' teachings, including the Beatitudes. It shows what Jesus expects of his followers.

server

A **server** is one who helps the celebrant at Mass or another sacrament.

share

To **share** means to give or receive the good things God has blessed us with. Jesus taught us to **share** our wealth, love, talents, and faith with each other.

sign of peace

During Mass we share the **sign of peace**. This handshake, hug, or kiss, and the words of greeting remind us to love our neighbors.

Sign of the Cross

In the name of the Father,

and of the Son,

and of the Holy Spirit.

Amen.

The **Sign of the Cross** is a prayer in honor of the Blessed Trinity. Using our right hand to make the shape of a cross on ourselves we say: "In the name of the Father, and of the Son, and of the Holy Spirit. Amen."

sin

A **sin** is a wrong choice we make that hurts others and ourselves. When we **sin** we turn away from God, although God continues to love us.

sister

A woman who joins a community of other women and makes special promises to God is a **sister**. **Sisters** dedicate their lives to prayer and service to God.

Son of God

Truly, this was the Son of God!

Son of God is a title for Jesus. It tells us that he is both God and human.

Stations of the Cross

The **Stations of the Cross** is a prayer that recalls the passion of Jesus. In churches there are usually fourteen pictures of **"stations"** that show different events on Jesus' way to his death on the cross.

stole

A **stole** is a long, narrow band of cloth worn around the necks of priests and bishops when celebrating the sacraments. A **stole** is a sign of ordination.

synagogue

A **synagogue** is place where Jewish people worship and learn.

Tt

tabernacle

A **tabernacle** is a cabinet where the blessed hosts, the Body of Christ, are kept.

temptation

A **temptation** is when we want to do something we should not do. It is common to feel **temptation**. It is wrong to give in to it.

100

Ten Commandments

I AM THE LORD YOUR GOD.

YOU SHALL NOT TAKE THE NAME OF THE LORD IN VAIN.

REMEMBER TO KEEP HOLY THE SABBATH DAY.

HONOR YOUR FATHER AND MOTHER.

YOU SHALL NOT KILL.

YOU SHALL NOT COMMIT ADULTERY.

YOU SHALL NOT STEAL.

YOU SHALL NOT TELL LIES ABOUT YOUR NEIGHBOR.

YOU SHALL NOT COVET YOUR NEIGHBOR'S WIFE.

YOU SHALL NOT COVET YOUR NEIGHBOR'S GOODS.

The **Ten Commandments** are the laws that God gave to Moses for the Israelites. Christians also read, study, and obey the **Ten Commandments** today as a way to lead a good life.

101

T t

tomb

A **tomb** is a place to put a dead body. Jesus' **tomb** was a cave.

transfiguration

Transfigure means to change appearance. One day Jesus' friends saw his face and clothes shining like the sun while he talked with the long-dead prophets Moses and Elijah. This event is called the **transfiguation.**

Trinity

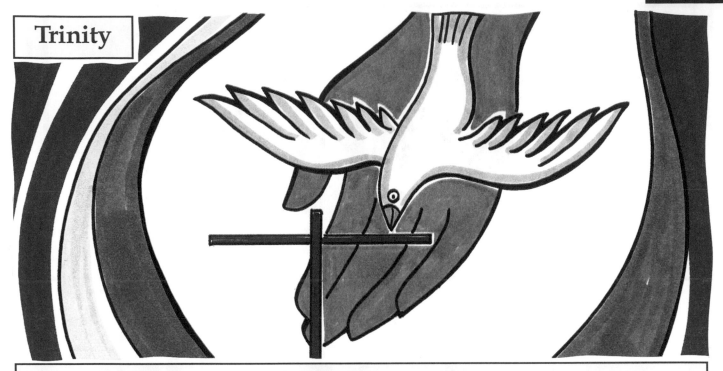

The **Trinity** is the way Christians describe the mystery of God: three persons in one God—the Father, the Son, and the Holy Spirit.

truth

Truth is what God desires of our lives. We can live **truthfully** by following Jesus, who called himself "the way, the **truth**, and the life."

103

unity

Unity is a feeling of being one with a group of people. The group's sharing of the same ideas and beliefs makes its **unity** strong.

104

unleavened

Unleavened bread is baked without yeast so that it does not rise. Jewish people use **unleavened** bread at Passover. Catholics use it for the Eucharist.

usher

An **usher** does helpful things during a worship service. An **usher** may help people find their seats and collect the offering from the people.

Vatican

The **Vatican** is a small city within Rome. It is the home for the pope and the headquarters for the Roman Catholic church.

vestments

Vestments are special clothes worn by ministers who celebrate or assist at Mass and other sacraments or worship services.

virtues

A **virtue** is a good habit that helps a person do what is right. The three most important **virtues** are faith, hope, and love.

vocation

Vocation means "a calling." A Christian **vocation** is a call from God to serve God's people. Everyone is given a **vocation** at Baptism.

Ww

water

Since we need **water** to live, it is a symbol for life. **Water** is used in church for blessings and for Baptism.

wine

Wine is a drink made from grapes. During Mass Jesus is present in the bread and **wine**.

wisdom

Wisdom is knowing how God wants us to live and trying to live that way.

wise men

In the Bible, the **wise men** were the three kings who visited the baby Jesus and honored him with gifts. They are also called the Magi.

witness

A **witness** is someone who tells, in words or actions, of the good news of Jesus Christ. The apostles were **witnesses** to Jesus' life and told others about him.

Word

The **Word** is another name for Jesus. His **words** are God's **words**. Jesus is also called the **Word** of God.

works of mercy

Works of mercy are things we do to help others. Feeding the hungry and comforting a friend who is sick are **works of mercy**.

worship

Worship is the act of praising and honoring God. For Catholics, the Mass is an example of public **worship**.

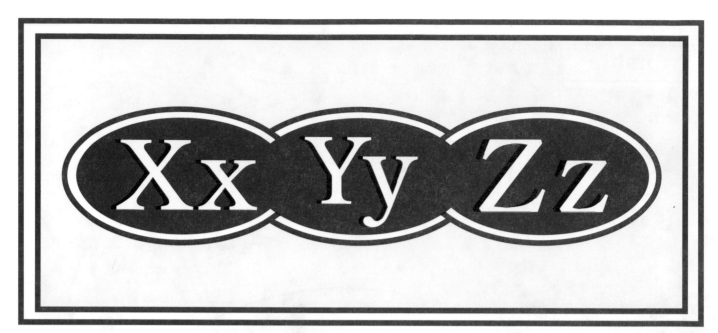

X (symbol)

X is the first letter of the Greek name for Christ. **P** is the second. Together (☧) they make a symbol, called Chi Rho, which is used to mean Jesus, the Christ.

Yahweh

Yahweh is a name of God, given to Moses in the desert. It means, "I am who I am." God is now, always has been, and always will be.

To

....

HAPPY EASTER

Love

....

THE EASTER BUNNY
is coming to
NEW JERSEY

Written by Eric James   Illustrated by Mari Lobo

The sweet Easter Bunny
is skipping along,
heading through New Jersey
singing this song:

ASBURY PARK
BOOKS

Cakes

"The eggs are delivered.
My Easter job's done.
And now it is time
that I joined in the fun!"

She jumps down a tunnel
that runs underground,
and pops up again
in each city and town.

Atlantic City, Princeton,
and Montclair, too.
I bet there's a tunnel
that's very near you!

In Elizabeth children have smiles on their faces, and eggs decorated like people and places!

But one little boy
drops the egg from his hands.
A loud **CRACKING** sound
can be heard as it lands.

"Oh dear!" says the bunny,
and dabs at a tear.
"You need cheering up
so thank goodness I'm here!"

She wiggles her ears,
she hops on the spot,
she waggles her tail,
and he giggles a lot!

In Trenton, there is
an Easter parade.
Most children are clapping
but one looks afraid.

That clapping is noisy.
These legs are so TALL!
It's crowded and loud,
and she's ever so small!

"Gee whiz, what a din!
I know just what to do.
Come here little one
and I'll hold hands with you!"

She wiggles her ears,
and spins her around.
The little girl laughs
as her feet leave the ground!

Down in Jersey City
while having a rest,
she eats Sweet Green Tomato Pie.
(It's the best!)

Across in the park
there's an egg-rolling race.
A small boy falls down
and he's now lost his place!

The bunny trips up
as she's going to help.
She falls down the hill
with an **OUCH** and a YELP!

YELP!

OUCH!

She's just a big blur
as she tumbles on past.
The boy runs to help her.
He's going so FAST!

FINISH

She wiggles her ears,
he can't (but he tries!).
They hop up and down
for they've just won first prize!

In Paterson, a girl's lost
her favorite stuffed bear.
Where could she have left him?
She's looked everywhere!

"When I'm feeling sad
do you know what I do?
I hop up and down!
Do you want to try too?"

She wiggles her ears, the girl thinks it's funny,
and laughs even more when she hops like a bunny!

They both jump around like they haven't a care.
And look what the chicks have just found, over there!

In Cape May, the bunny
helps children with SHARING.

In Hoboken, she helps a sweet child
to be DARING.

In Toms River she SINGS,
in New Brunswick she WIGGLES.

Wherever she goes
she brings LAUGHTER and GIGGLES!

This day's been so busy
but also such fun.
The bunny daydreams
in the warm setting sun.

The twilight is coming,
the three chicks are lazing,
and tweeting about
how this day's been #AMAZING!

The bunny jumps up,
snapping out of her daze,
"There's only three-hundred-
and-sixty-four days!"

More chocolate needs making!
New eggs will need wrapping!
It's all so exciting,
the three chicks start flapping!

"New Jersey's great and we love being here. We'll make lots more eggs and we'll be back next year!"

She wrinkles her nose,
she wiggles her ears,
she blows you a kiss,
and she just...disappears!

Written by Eric James
Illustrated by Mari Lobo
Additional artwork by Barbara Szepesi Szucs
Designed by Nicky Scott

Published by Sourcebooks Wonderland,
an imprint of Sourcebooks Kids
P.O. Box 4410, Naperville, Illinois 60567-4410
(630) 961-3900
sourcebookskids.com

Date of Production: August 2019
Run Number: 5015369
Printed and bound in China (1010)
10 9 8 7 6 5 4 3 2 1